PEANUTS
GUIDE TO LIFE

By Charles M. Schulz

RUNNING PRESS
PHILADELPHIA · LONDON ·

Running Press Book Publishers
125 South Twenty-second Street
Philadelphia, Pennsylvania 19103-4399
Visit us on the web at www.runningpress.com.

Cover and interior design by Gwen Galeone.
Edited by Deborah Grandinetti

This edition published in 2007 under license from Running Press Book Publishers,
exclusively for Hallmark Cards, Inc.

Published by Hallmark Books,
a division of Hallmark Cards, Inc.,
Kansas City, MO 64141
Visit us on the Web at www.Hallmark.com.

ISBN: 978-1-59530-123-9
BOK2081

Printed and bound in China

TABLE OF CONTENTS

F O R E W O R D

I t has been the prerogative of the humorist throughout history to look closely at life, chew it over, and spit the observations back out in a way that's guaranteed to tickle the funnybone. This was probably as true for the cave dwellers as it is in the computer age. I can't imagine how any society could thrive without the benefit of those folks gifted at reflecting back the human condition—the hope, the joy, the fear—and helping us see the hilarity of it all. Humorists do more than make us laugh, however. They also force us to stop and *think*.

This has always been true for Charles M. Schulz. I have followed his work closely over the years, and have always enjoyed his comical and ingenious observations. The *Peanuts Guide to Life* captures his insights and his life philosophy, as reflected through the medium of his world-famous comic strip, "Peanuts." The comic strip and its beloved characters appeared in over 2,300 newspapers and more than 1,400 books. Animated television specials based on his characters won prestigious Peabody and Emmy awards.

Schulz came from humble beginnings, but it seems he was always destined to be a cartoonist. He was born in Minneapolis, Minnesota on November 26, 1922. His uncle called him "Sparky" after a horse in the comic strip of the day, "Barney Google." So, even as a baby, little "Sparky" was linked to the social and humorous commentary of the comic strips. When Charles was age four, someone gave him a blackboard that had a roll of paper on top, printed with the alphabet. That chalkboard grew to be one of his best friends. He used it to draw hundreds of pictures.

A shy boy, Schulz insulated himself from the cares of the world with his family, his drawing, and his love for books, music, and the arts. By the time the "Peanuts" comic strip first appeared on October 2, 1950, the characters had already helped to shape Schulz's creative and professional life. Eventually, they would propel him into the public eye, as children and adults around the world grew to know and love

Charlie Brown, Snoopy, Lucy, Linus, Sally Brown, and the other Peanuts characters

The comic strips, or the "funny papers" as they were called by many people, were so much a part of Charles Schulz's life and my own. I would often turn to the comics to study them intensely, laugh aloud at the clever content, or simply smile as I attempted to extract meaning from the narrative art form. Comics are uniquely a part of American life and culture, providing us with an entertaining topic of discussion at the dinner table, the office water cooler, and in lunchrooms and boardrooms of the country. Herb Galewitz, in the book, *Great Comics*, suggested that comics were, "in a sense the forerunners of the radio soap operas of yesterday and the TV situation comedies of today."

This book, *Peanuts Guide to Life*, takes a different approach than most others by Charles M. Schulz. Instead of providing cartoon "stories," *Peanuts Guide to Life* is full of lessons about how to succeed in the emotional and social sphere of life, and how to use plain old common sense. I am certain that you will enjoy how the Schulz' characteristic humor stays with you throughout your daily tasks. His down-to-earth and practical philosophies, illustrated colorfully and whimsically, will speak directly to you about such things as confidence, self-reliance, effort, love, and other real life issues. Although this book, like comic strips, comes to you in a small package, it is filled with a large sense of humor and big ideas.

Charles M. Schulz, one of the greatest cartoonists of our time, was an expert of this creative art. From his creative genius came a comic strip that was simply called "Peanuts," which touched the lives of many of its readers, including my own. We are all the richer for the view of the world as seen through the eyes of the "Peanuts" characters. In the words of Snoopy:

Keep looking up...
That's the secret of Life....

Bill Cosby, EdD with Gordon Berry, EdD
New York, N.Y.
2004

Life Philosophy

"LIFE IS LIKE AN ICE CREAM CONE. . .
YOU HAVE TO LEARN TO LICK IT!"

Charlie Brown

"AS SOON AS A CHILD IS BORN,
HE OR SHE SHOULD BE ISSUED
A DOG AND A BANJO..."

Charlie Brown

"THEY SAY IF YOU BECOME
A BETTER PERSON, YOU'LL HAVE
A BETTER LIFE..."

Charlie Brown

"IF YOU TRY TO BE A BETTER DOG,
SOMETIMES YOU GET AN
EXTRA COOKIE..."

Snoopy

"I HAVE A PHILOSOPHY THAT HAS BEEN REFINED IN THE FIRES OF HARDSHIP AND STRUGGLE... 'LIVE AND LET LIVE!'"

Lucy

"A LIFE SHOULD BE PLANNED INNING BY INNING."

Peppermint Patty

Confidence

"IT'S BETTER TO LIVE ONE DAY AS A LION THAN A DOZEN YEARS AS A SHEEP."

Snoopy

"IF EVERYBODY AGREED WITH **ME**, THEY'D ALL BE RIGHT!"

Lucy

"KEEP LOOKING UP. . .
THAT'S THE SECRET OF LIFE. . ."

Snoopy

"WHEN YOU GO SOME PLACE NICE, YOU SHOULD ALWAYS SHINE YOUR FEET!"

Snoopy

"'ALL IS WELL'. . . THAT'S MY NEW PHILOSOPHY. . ."

Sally

Self-Care

I SIGNED UP FOR A SUMMER READING PROGRAM AT THE LIBRARY...

GOD DIDN'T MAKE THE SUN FOR YOU TO SIT IN THE LIBRARY, MARCIE

YOU KNOW MORE ABOUT THEOLOGY THAN I THOUGHT, SIR

© 1990 United Feature Syndicate, Inc.

"SOMETIMES ALL WE NEED IS
A LITTLE PAMPERING TO HELP
US FEEL BETTER..."

Linus

"INSULATE THE OL' ATTIC!"

Snoopy

"MOST PSYCHIATRISTS AGREE THAT
SITTING IN A PUMPKIN PATCH
IS EXCELLENT THERAPY FOR
A TROUBLED MIND!"

Linus

Self-Reliance

"IF YOU WANT SOMETHING DONE RIGHT,
YOU SHOULD DO IT YOURSELF!"

Snoopy

"WELL FROM NOW ON, LINUS,
THINK FOR YOURSELF. . . DON'T TAKE
ANY ADVICE FROM ANYONE!"

Charlie Brown

"WHO CARES WHAT OTHER PEOPLE THINK?"

Sally

"YOU CAN'T BELIEVE EVERYTHING
YOU HEAR, YOU KNOW. . ."

Schroeder

People Skills

"IF YOU CAN'T BEAT 'EM,
COOPERATE 'EM TO DEATH!"

Charlie Brown

"IN FIRST-AID CLASS I LEARNED
THAT IF YOU HAVE OFFENDED SOMEONE,
THE BEST TREATMENT IS TO APOLOGIZE
IMMEDIATELY. . ."

Marcie

"THE AVERAGE DAD NEEDS
LOTS OF ENCOURAGEMENT."

Charlie Brown

"WHEN YOU GET A COMPLIMENT,
ALL YOU HAVE TO SAY IS 'THANK YOU.'"

Classmate talking to Rerun

Prudence

"IT'S A MISTAKE TO TRY TO AVOID
THE UNPLEASANT THINGS IN LIFE...
BUT I'M BEGINNING TO CONSIDER IT..."

Charlie Brown

"I'VE GOT TO STOP THIS BUSINESS
OF TALKING WITHOUT THINKING. . ."

Linus

"A PERSON HAS TO BE CAREFUL
ABOUT THINGS HE MIGHT REGRET
YEARS FROM NOW."

Linus

"THERE'S NO SENSE IN DOING A LOT
OF BARKING IF YOU DON'T REALLY
HAVE ANYTHING TO SAY"

Snoopy

Wisdom

"I HAVE OBSERVED THAT WHENEVER
YOU TRY TO HIT SOMEBODY, THERE IS
A TENDENCY FOR THEM TO
TRY TO HIT YOU BACK."

Charlie Brown

"WHENEVER IT'S ONE MAN AGAINST
AN INSTITUTION, THERE IS ALWAYS A
TENDENCY FOR THE INSTITUTION TO WIN!"

Charlie Brown

"NEVER TRY TO LICK ICE CREAM
OFF A HOT SIDEWALK!"

Snoopy

"NEVER TRY TO EAT A SUGAR-SANDWICH
ON A WINDY DAY!"

Charlie Brown

"NEVER TAKE ANY ADVICE THAT YOU
CAN UNDERSTAND. . . IT CAN'T POSSIBLY
BE ANY GOOD!"

Lucy

"NEVER JUMP INTO A PILE OF LEAVES
HOLDING A WET SUCKER!"

Linus

Effort

"IF YOU DON'T PLAY EVERY DAY, YOU LOSE THAT FINE EDGE..."

Snoopy

"SOME OF MY BEST TERM PAPERS
HAVE BEEN WRITTEN
BEFORE BREAKFAST!"

Sally

"NO ONE NEED EVER BE ASHAMED
OF FINGERNAILS MADE DIRTY BY
A HARD DAY'S WORK."

Linus

"JOHN RUSKIN ONCE WROTE
'THE BEST GRACE IS THE CONSCIOUSNESS
THAT WE HAVE EARNED OUR DINNER.'"

Linus

"GOOD COOKIES COME
WHEN THEY'RE CALLED."

Snoopy

"IT'S AMAZING HOW STUPID
YOU CAN BE WHEN YOU'RE IN LOVE..."

Lucy

"**GIVING**! THE ONLY REAL JOY IS **GIVING**!"

Charlie Brown

"LOVE IS NOT KNOWING WHAT
YOU'RE TALKING ABOUT."

Lucy

"WHEN NO ONE LOVES YOU, YOU HAVE TO PRETEND THAT EVERYONE LOVES YOU!"

Sally

"LOVE MAKES YOU DO STRANGE THINGS..."

Charlie Brown

Life's Little
Quirks

"A HOT DOG JUST DOESN'T TASTE RIGHT WITHOUT A BALL GAME IN FRONT OF IT!"

Charlie Brown

"THAT'S LIFE . . . PEOPLE GO AWAY,
AND DOGS STAY HOME . . ."

Charlie Brown

"I GUESS BABYSITTERS ARE LIKE
USED CARS. . . YOU NEVER REALLY KNOW
WHAT YOU'RE GETTING. . ."

Schroeder

"A WATCHED SUPPER DISH NEVER FILLS!"

Snoopy

"THERE'S NOTHING THAT CAN HARM
A PERSON MORE THAN TOO MUCH
FORMAL EDUCATION!"

Linus

"IT'S IMPOSSIBLE TO BE GLOOMY WHEN YOU'RE SITTING BEHIND A MARSHMALLOW . . ."

Lucy

"LIFE HAS ITS SUNSHINE AND ITS RAIN, SIR. . . ITS DAYS AND ITS NIGHTS. . . ITS PEAKS AND ITS VALLEYS. . ."

Marcie

"IN THE BOOK OF LIFE,
THE ANSWERS ARE NOT IN THE BACK!"

Charlie Brown